Sale Surname

Ireland: 1600s to 1900s

From Ireland Church Records of Baptism, Marriage and Death

Comprised of Roman Catholic and Church of Ireland Records

From Counties Carlow, Cork, Kerry and Dublin City

Compiled by **Donovan Hurst**

April 2, 2013

Dedication

This work is dedicated to all of those that came before us and shaped our lives to make us the people that we are today.

Table of Contents

Introduction

This is a compilation of individuals who have the surname of Sale that lived in the country of Ireland from the 1600s to the 1900s. I have placed each entry into one of four categories: Families, Individual Births/Baptisms, Individual Burials, and Individual Marriages. If a marriage entry primarily concerns an Individual Sale whom is female, then I have placed that entry under the category of Individual Marriages. If a marriage entry primarily concerns an Individual Sale whom is male, then I have placed that entry under the category of Families. Images of many of these listings are available at http://churchrecords.irishgenealogy.ie/churchrecords/.

To help guide the reader of this work, the format of this book is as follows:

- Main Family Entry (Husband and Wife) (Father and Mother)

  o Child of Main Family Entry, including Spouse(s) when available

    ▪ Grandchild of Main Family Entry, including Spouse(s) when available

      • Great-Grandchild of Main Family Entry, including Spouse(s) when available

(**Bolded Text**) following any entry includes any additional information such as Residence(s), Occupation(s), Signature(s), etc. when available.

Hurst

Some of the fonts used in this work symbolizes Celtic writing. The traditional letters, numbers, and punctuation marks and their Celtic counterparts are as follows:

Traditional Letters (Uppercase & Lowercase)

A a B b C c D d E f G g H h I i J j K k L l M m N n O o P p Q q R r S s T t U u V v W w X x Y y Z z

Celtic Letters (Uppercase & Lowercase)

A a B b C c D ð E e F ꜰ G g H h I i J j K k L l M m

N n O o P p Q q R r S s T t U u V v W w X x Y y Z z

Traditional Numbers

1 2 3 4 5 6 7 8 9 10

Celtic Numbers

1 2 3 4 5 6 7 8 9 10

Traditional Punctuation

. , : ' " & - ( )

Celtic Punctuation

. , : ' " & - ( )

Parish Churches

Carlow (Church of Ireland)

Dunleckney Parish and Wells Parish.

Cork & Ross (Roman Catholic or RC)

Carrigaline & Templebrigid Parish and Cork - South Parish.

Dublin (Church of Ireland)

Arbour Hill Barracks Parish, Clontarf Parish, Irishtown Parish, Sandford Parish, St. Anne Parish, St. Bride Parish, St. Catherine Parish, St. George Parish, St. James Parish, St. John Parish, St. Luke Parish, St. Mark Parish, St. Mary Parish, St. Matthias Parish, St. Michan Parish, St. Nicholas Without Parish, St. Paul Parish, and St. Peter Parish.

Dublin (Roman Catholic or RC)

Rathmines Parish, SS. Michael & John Parish, St. Agatha Parish, St. Andrew Parish, St. Audoen Parish. St. Catherine Parish, St. Lawrence Parish, St. Mary Parish, St. Mary, Pro Cathedral Parish, St. Michan Parish, and St. Nicholas Parish.

Kerry (Church of Ireland)

Ballymacelligott & Ballyseedy Parish and Castleisland Parish.

Kerry (Roman Catholic or R)

Abbeydorney Parish, Ballybunion Parish, Causeway Parish, Killarney Parish, Listowel Parish, and Tralee Parish .

Families

- Charles Sale & Unknown Sale

  o Charles Sale – bapt. 19 Sep 1632 (Baptism, **St. John Parish**)

  o Hester Sale – bapt. 30 Nov 1634 (Baptism, **St. John Parish**)

- Edward Sale & Bridget Dixon

  o William Edward Sale – b. 23 Aug 1874, bapt. 31 Aug 1874 (Baptism, **St. Michan Parish (RC)**)

  o Mary Elizabeth Sale – b. 24 Jul 1880, bapt. 30 Jul 1880 (Baptism, **St. Mary, Pro Cathedral Parish (RC)**)

Edward Sale (father):

Residence - 63 Wellington Street - August 31, 1874

33 Cole's Lane - July 30, 1880

- Edward Sale & Elizabeth Bergin

  o Elizabeth Anne De Sale – b. 1877, bapt. 1877 (Baptism, **St. Andrew Parish (RC)**)

Edward Sale (father):

Residence - 30 Deuzille Street - 1877

Also Known As - Edward De Sale

- Edward Sale & Elizabeth Keenan

  o Anne Sale – bapt. 18 Jul 1806 (Baptism, **St. Michan Parish (RC)**)

Hurst

- Edward Sale & Louisa Sale

  - Elizabeth Sale – b. 12 Apr 1899, bapt. 25 Jun 1899 (Baptism, **Arbour Hill Barracks Parish**)

Edward Sale (father):

Residence - 4 Married Quarters, Arbour Hill Barracks - June 25, 1899

Occupation - Driver, A. S. Corps - June 25, 1899

- George Sale & Elizabeth Unknown

  - John Sale – bapt. 8 Dec 1799 (Baptism, **St. Catherine Parish**)

- Gregory Sale & Mary Walsh – 18 Jan 1801 (Marriage, **St. Nicholas Parish (RC)**)

  - Eleanor Sale – bapt. 1802 (Baptism, **St. Andrew Parish (RC)**)

  - Gulielmo Sale – bapt. Jan 1813 (Baptism, **St. Nicholas Parish (RC)**)

Wedding Witnesses:

Anne Freeman & Austin Keenan

- Harvey Sale & Rebecca Unknown

  - Jeffrey Sale – bapt. 30 Oct 1706 (Baptism, **St. Nicholas Without Parish**)

  - John Sale – bapt. 3 Apr 1709 (Baptism, **St. Nicholas Without Parish**)

  - John Sale – bapt. 13 Nov 1711 (Baptism, **St. Nicholas Without Parish**)

Harvey Sale (father):

Residence - New Row - October 30, 1706

April 3, 1709

November 13, 1711

Sale Surname Ireland: 1600s to 1900s

- Henry Sale & Bridget Rahily – 29 Apr 1843 (Marriage, **Abbeydorney Parish (RC)**)

  - Thomas Sale – b. 13 Apr 1845, bapt 13 Apr 1845 (Baptism, **Causeway Parish (RC)**)

Henry Sale (father):

Residence - Dromartin - April 13, 1845

Wedding Witnesses:

Patrick Rahily & Timothy McCarthy

- Henry Sale & Elizabeth Sale

  - Henry Sale – b. 20 Nov 1818, bapt. 6 Dec 1818 (Baptism, **St. George Parish**)

- Henry Sale & Ellen Branagan

  - John Sale – b. 6 Dec 1858, bapt. 15 Dec 1858 (Baptism, **St. Nicholas Parish (RC)**)

  - Mary Anne Sale – b. 28 Dec 1861, bapt. 10 Jan 1862 (Baptism, **St. Nicholas Parish (RC)**)

Henry Sale (father):

Residence - 31 Cuffe Street - December 15, 1858

3 Charlotte Street - January 10, 1862

- Henry Sale & Ellen Connor

  - Jane Sale – b. 15 Aug 1846, bapt. 15 Aug 1846 (Baptism, **Causeway Parish (RC)**)

Henry Sale (father):

Residence - Addergown - August 15, 1846

Hurst

- Henry Sale & Helen Mahony
  - Morgan Sale – b. 8 Apr 1837, bapt. 8 Apr 1837 (Baptism, *Causeway Parish* (RC))
  - John Sale – b. 4 Feb 1844, bapt. 4 Feb 1844 (Baptism, *Causeway Parish* (RC))

Henry Sale (father):

Residence - Heart Hill - April 8, 1837

Addergown - February 4, 1844

- Henry Sale & Mary Enright
  - Ellen Sale – b. 24 Feb 1873, bapt. 2 Mar 1873 (Baptism, *Causeway Parish* (RC))

Henry Sale (father):

Residence - Lacca - March 2, 1873

- James Sale & Catherine Slattery
  - Honor Sale – b. 16 Jul 1843, bapt. 16 Jul 1843 (Baptism, *Causeway Parish* (RC))

James Sale (father):

Residence - Heart Hill - July 16, 1843

- James Sale & Mary Unknown
  - John Sale – bapt. 24 May 1752 (Baptism, *St. Catherine Parish*)
- James Sale & Unknown
  - Allison Sale [written as Alson] (Daughter) – bur. 5 Dec 1641 (Burial, *St. Michan Parish*)

Sale Surname Ireland: 1600s to 1900s

- John Sale & Bridget Flannigan – 1 Jan 1844 (Marriage, **Causeway Parish (RC)**)

  o Honor Sale – b. 2 Mar 1845, bapt. 2 Mar 1845 (Baptism, **Causeway Parish (RC)**)

John Sale (father):

  Residence - **Dromartin - March 2, 1845**

Bridget Flannigan (mother):

  Residence - **Heart Hill - January 1, 1844**

Wedding Witnesses:

Henry Sale

- John Sale & Catherine Shaughnessy

  o Gerard Sale – b. 1 Jan 1879, bapt. 3 Jan 1879 (Baptism, **Causeway Parish (RC)**)

John Sale (father):

  Residence - **Acres - January 3, 1879**

- John Sale & Dorothy Sale

  o William Sale – bapt. 24 Jun 1734 (Baptism, **St. Catherine Parish**)

- John Sale & Eleanor Unknown

  o Edmund Sale – bapt. 22 Dec 1695 (Baptism, **St. Nicholas Without Parish**)

John Sale (father):

  Residence - **New Row - December 22, 1695**

Hurst

- John Sale & Mary Barrett

  - Henry Sale – b. 4 Dec 1827, bapt. 4 Dec 1827 (Baptism, **Tralee Parish (RC)**)

John Sale (father):

Residence - Tralee - December 4, 1827

- John Sale & Mary Conyann – 26 Dec 1855 (Marriage, **St. Mary Parish (RC)**)

Wedding Witnesses:

William Grimley & Mary Conyann

- John Sale & Mary Cooke

  - Samuel Sale & Margaret O'Sullivan – 15 Apr 1879 (Marriage, **Killarney Parish (RC)**)

Samuel Sale (son):

Residence - Dublin - April 15, 1879

Margaret O'Sullivan, daughter of Michael O'Sullivan & Bridget Cronin

(daughter-in-law):

Residence - Cloghereen - April 15, 1879

Wedding Witnesses:

Rev. Unknown McCarthy & Disey Murphy

- John Sale & Mary Anne Cooke

  - Catherine Sale – b. 5 Jan 1860, bapt. 25 Jan 1860 (Baptism, **St. Mary, Pro Cathedral Parish (RC)**)

Sale Surname Ireland: 1600s to 1900s

John Sale (father):

Residence - 13 Capel Street - January 25, 1860

- John Sale & Mary Mackey – 24 Sep 1841 (Marriage, **St. Mary, Pro Cathedral Parish** (RC))

Wedding Witnesses:

John Byrne & Isabel Elliott

- John Sale & Mary Sale
    - Peter Sale & Catherine Quinn – 1 Aug 1858 (Marriage, **St. Agatha Parish** (RC))
        - Mary Elizabeth Sale – b. 18 May 1859, bapt. 23 May 1859 (Baptism, **St. Agatha Parish** (RC))
        - Joseph Patrick Sale – b. 24 Apr 1861, bapt. 29 Apr 1861 (Baptism, **St. Agatha Parish** (RC))
        - Helen Mary Sale – b. 29 Nov 1863, bapt. 4 Dec 1863 (Baptism, **St. Agatha Parish** (RC))
        - Peter Matthew Sale – b. 8 Apr 1866, bapt. 11 Apr 1866 (Baptism, **St. Mary, Pro Cathedral Parish** (RC))

Peter Sale (son):

Residence - 14 William Place - August 1, 1858

May 23, 1859

April 29, 1861

December 4, 1863

4 Dorset Lane - April 11, 1866

Catherine Quinn, daughter of Richard Quinn & Elizabeth Unknown (daughter-in-law):

Residence - 14 William Place - August 1, 1858

Hurst

Wedding Witnesses:

Mark Quinn & Bridget Quinn

- John Sale & Mary Unknown

  - Richard Sale – bapt. 1804 (Baptism, **St. Andrew Parish (RC)**)

- John Sale & Mary Walsh

  - Honor Sale – b. 1 May 1844, bapt. 1 May 1844 (Baptism, **Causeway Parish (RC)**)

John Sale (father):

Residence - Heart Hill - May 1, 1844

- John Sale & Unknown

  - John Sale & Anne McCabe – 1 Apr 1883 (Marriage, **St. Andrew Parish (RC)**)

    - Catherine Sale – b. 8 Nov 1889, bapt. 11 Nov 1889 (Baptism, **SS. Michael & John Parish (RC)**)

John Sale (son):

Residence - 3 Chatham Row - April 1, 1883

28 Stephen's Street - November 11, 1889

Anne McCabe, daughter of Cornelius McCabe (daughter-in-law):

Residence - 3 Chatham Row - April 1, 1883

Wedding Witnesses:

Francis Mason & Anne Edwards

Sale Surname Ireland: 1600s to 1900s

- John Henry James Sale & Unknown

  o John Henry James Sale & Sophia Sovereign Marshall – 5 Oct 1855 (Marriage, **St. Paul Parish**)

Signatures:

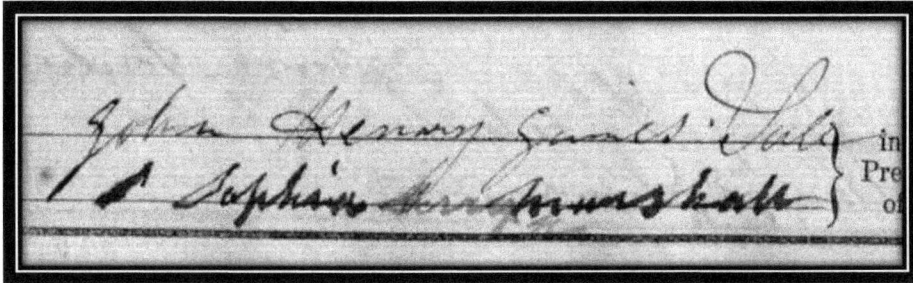

John Henry James Sale (son):

    Residence - Royal Barracks - October 5, 1855

    Occupation - Private, 2nd Queen's Royal Regiment - October 5, 1855

Sophia Sovereign Marshall, daughter of Robert Marshall (daughter-in-law):

    Residence - Irwin Street - October 5, 1855

    Relationship Status at Marriage - minor

Robert Marshall (father):

    Occupation - Publican

John Henry James Sale (father):

    Occupation - Wine Merchant

Hurst

Wedding Witnesses:

Thomas Browning & Mary Nevin

Signatures:

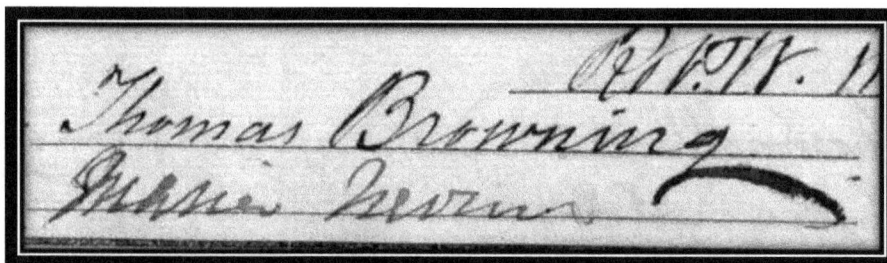

- Joseph Sale & Mary Anne Carpenter

  o Elizabeth Sale – bapt. 1838 (Baptism, **St. Mary Parish** (RC))

  o Hannah Sale – bapt. 1856 (Baptism, **St. Mary Parish** (RC))

  o Mary Jane Sale – bapt. 1859 (Baptism, **St. Mary Parish** (RC))

  o Elizabeth Sale – bapt. 1862 (Baptism, **St. Mary Parish** (RC))

  o John Sale – bapt. 1864 (Baptism, **St. Mary Parish** (RC))

  o Richard Sale – b. 1867, bapt. 1867 (Baptism, **St. Mary Parish** (RC))

- Matthew Sale & Amelia Unknown

  o Susanna Sale – b. Jan 1817, bur. 12 Aug 1818 (Burial, **Clontarf Parish**)

Susanna Sale (daughter):

Residence - Dublin City, St. James Parish, Co. Dublin - before August 12, 1818

Age at Death - 20 months

  o Amelia Sale – b. 5 Feb 1824, bapt. 17 Mar 1824 (Baptism, **St. James Parish**)

  o Mary Elizabeth Sale – bapt. 14 Mar 1830 (Baptism, **St. Mary Parish**)

Sale Surname Ireland: 1600s to 1900s

o   Thomas Sale & Margaret Louisa Campbell – 29 Jun 1845 (Marriage, **St. Mark Parish**)

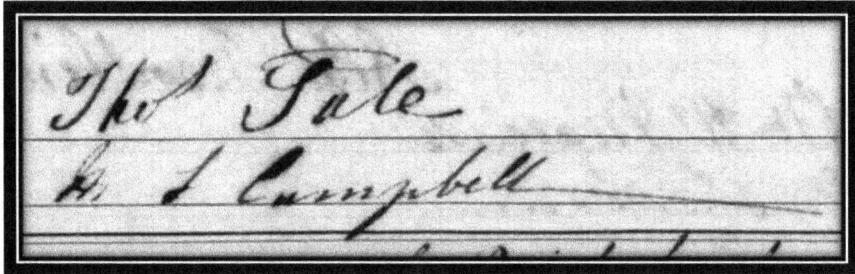

Signatures:

- Eleanor Sale – b. 14 May 1846, bapt. 29 May 1846 (Baptism, **St. Mary Parish**)

Thomas Sale (son):

Residence - Cumberland - June 29, 1845

42 Jervis Street - May 29, 1846

Occupation - Cabinet Maker - June 29, 1845

May 29, 1846

Margaret Louisa Campbell, daughter of Jacob Campbell (daughter):

Residence - Cumberland - June 29, 1845

Jacob Campbell (father):

Occupation - Carpenter

Matthew Sale (father):

Occupation - Cabinet Maker

Wedding Witnesses:

Thomas Wells & Henry Magrath

Signatures:

- o   Emily Sale & Martin Fahey – 31 May 1849 (Marriage, **St. George Parish**)

Signatures:

Emily Sale (father):

 Residence - 8 Middle Gardiner Street - May 31, 1849

Martin Fahey, son of John Fahey (son-in-law):

 Residence - 8 Middle Gardiner Street - May 31, 1849

 Occupation - Servant - May 31, 1849

John Fahey (father):

 Occupation - Farmer

Sale Surname Ireland: 1600s to 1900s

Matthew Sale (father):

Occupation - Cabinet Maker

Wedding Witnesses:

Margaret Flood & J. Edmiston

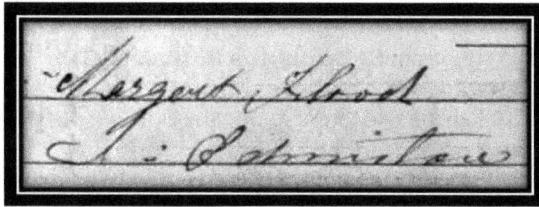

Signatures:

Matthew Sale (father):

Residence - Dolphin's Barn - March 17, 1824

10 Lotts - March 14, 1830

Occupation - Cabinet Maker - March 17, 1824

March 14, 1830

- Matthew Sale & Catherine Sale
  - Patrick Sale – bapt. 17 Mar 1740 (Baptism, **St. Mary Parish**)
- Matthew John Sale & Anne Crosby – 25 Feb 1809 (Marriage, **St. Andrew Parish (RC)**)

Wedding Witnesses:

Gulielmo Mason & Anne Sale

- Patrick Sale & Alice Unknown
  - Jane Sale – bapt. Jun 1699 (Baptism, **St. Nicholas Without Parish**)

Hurst

Patrick Sale (father):

Residence - New Row - June 1699

- Patrick Sale & Teresa Browne

  - Patrick Sale – bapt. 14 Jun 1848 (Baptism, **St. Nicholas Parish (RC)**)

- Patrick Sale & Teresa Pardue

  - Mary Anne Sale – bapt. 20 Oct 1845 (Baptism, **St. Nicholas Parish (RC)**)

  - Christopher Sale & Sarah Butler – 10 Feb 1866 (Marriage, **St. Nicholas Parish (RC)**)

    - Mary Sale – b. 6 Dec 1871, bapt. 13 Dec 1871 (Baptism, **St. Catherine Parish (RC)**)

    - Patrick Sale – b. 23 Apr 1875, bapt. 28 Apr 1875 (Baptism, **St. Catherine Parish (RC)**)

    - Catherine Sale – b. 13 Jan 1880, bapt. Jan 1880 (Baptism, **St. Catherine Parish (RC)**)

Christopher Sale (son):

Residence - 13 Skinner's Alley - February 10, 1866

103 Thomas Street - December 13, 1871

6 Engine Alley - April 28, 1875

January 1880

Sarah Butler, daughter of John Butler & Sarah Unknown (daughter-in-law):

Residence - 13 Skinner's Alley - February 10, 1866

Wedding Witnesses:

Gulielmo Ferguson & Frances Ferguson

- James Sale – bapt. 10 Jun 1850 (Baptism, **St. Nicholas Parish (RC)**)

- Patrick Sale – b. 17 Mar 1861, bapt. 25 Mar 1861 (Baptism, **St. Nicholas Parish (RC)**)

Sale Surname Ireland: 1600s to 1900s

- o Mary Sale – b. 18 Aug 1864, bapt. 19 Aug 1864 (Baptism, **St. Catherine Parish** (RC))

- o Teresa Sale – b. 18 Aug 1864, bapt. 19 Aug 1864 (Baptism, **St. Catherine Parish** (RC))

Patrick Sale (father):

Residence - 20 Francis Street - March 25, 1861

5 Engine Alley - August 19, 1864

- Peter Sale & Anne Sale

  - o Mary Sale – bapt. 20 Jun 1831 (Baptism, **St. Mary, Pro Cathedral Parish** (RC))

- Richard Sale & Margaret Dowling – 11 Jul 1847 (Marriage, **St. Audoen Parish** (RC))

Wedding Witnesses:

Michael Dowling & Margaret Dowling

- Robert Sale & Deborah Sale

  - o Anne Sale – b. 3 Jun 1822, bapt. 23 Jun 1822 (Baptism, **St. George Parish**)

- Robert Sale & Mary Doyne – 22 Feb 1846 (Marriage, **St. Mary, Pro Cathedral Parish** (RC))

  - o Edward Sale – b. 1849, bapt. 1849 (Baptism, **St. Andrew Parish** (RC))

Wedding Witnesses:

William David & Mary Davis

- Robert Milton Sale & Deborah Colclough – 30 Oct 1808 (Marriage, **St. Mark Parish**)

  - o Anne Sale – bapt. Mar 1811 (Baptism, **St. Catherine Parish** (RC))

  - o Sarah Sale – bapt. Mar 1811 (Baptism, **St. Catherine Parish** (RC))

Hurst

- Robert Milton Sale & Anne Connolly – 5 Jun 1836 (Marriage, **St. George Parish**)

Signature:

Signatures (Marriage):

Robert Milton Sale (husband):

Residence - George's Place, St. George Parish - June 5, 1836

Occupation - Gentleman - June 5, 1836

Anne Connolly (wife):

Residence - George's Place, St. George Parish - June 5, 1836

Occupation - Spinster - June 5, 1836

Wedding Witnesses:

Robert Egam & Edward A. McEntie

Signatures:

Sale Surname Ireland: 1600s to 1900s

- Robert Nelson Sale & Anne Unknown

  - Charles Sale – bapt. 1837 (Baptism, **St. Andrew Parish (RC)**)

- Samuel Sale & Elizabeth Sale

  - John Sale – b. 1812, bapt. 25 Oct 1812 (Baptism, **St. Catherine Parish**)

  - Sarah Sale – b. 20 Sep 1816, bapt. 13 Oct 1816 (Baptism, **St. Catherine Parish**)

Samuel Sale (father):

Residence - Chanel Street - 1816

- Samuel Sale & Margaret Sullivan

  - Cherry Mary Sale – b. 11 Jan 1880, bapt. 12 Jan 1880 (Baptism, **St. Lawrence Parish (RC)**)

  - Anne Josephine Sale – b. 16 Dec 1880, bapt. 29 Dec 1880 (Baptism, **St. Lawrence Parish (RC)**)

  - Henry Joseph Sale – b. 13 Jul 1882, bapt. 21 Jul 1882 (Baptism, **St. Agatha Parish (RC)**)

Samuel Sale (father):

Residence - 5 Hoey's Avenue, North Strand - January 12, 1880

130 North Strand - December 29, 1880

32 Ballybough Road - July 21, 1882

- Samuel Sale & Unknown

  o Angelina Sale & Thomas Ledwich Tyrrell – 19 Dec 1870 (Marriage, **St. Mary Parish**)

Signatures:

Angelina Sale (daughter):

   Residence - 107 Upper Dorset Street - December 19, 1870

Thomas Ledwich Tyrrell, son of Thomas Tyrrell (son-in-law):

   Residence - Cloyton, Co. Kildare - December 19, 1870

   Occupation - Esquire - December 19, 1870

Thomas Tyrrell (father):

   Occupation - Barrister at Law

Samuel Sale (father):

   Occupation - Esquire

Sale Surname Ireland: 1600s to 1900s

Wedding Witnesses:

Samuel William Sale & Gregory Sale

Signatures:

- o Gregory Sale & Adelaide Frances L'Estrange – 28 Apr 1880 (Marriage, **St. George Parish**)

  - ▪ Adelaide Constance L'Estrange Sale – b. 25 Mar 1881, bapt. 27 Apr 1881 (Baptism, **St. Matthias**

    Parish)

Signature:

Signatures (Marriage):

Hurst

Gregory Sale (son):

Residence - Newpark, Naas Parish, Co. Kildare - April 28, 1880

Newpark, Naas Parish - April 27, 1881

Occupation - Esquire, Medical Doctor - April 28, 1880

Medical Doctor - April 27, 1881

Adelaide Frances L'Estrange, daughter of Guy P. L'Estrange (daughter-in-law):

Residence - 25 Eccles Street, Rathangan, Glebe Parish, Co. Kildare - April 28, 1880

Guy P. L'Estrange (father):

Signature:

Occupation - Clerk in Holy Orders

Samuel Sale (father):

Occupation - Esquire

Sale Surname Ireland: 1600s to 1900s

Wedding Witnesses:

Guy P. L'Estrange & Thomas Ridgeway Sale

Signatures:

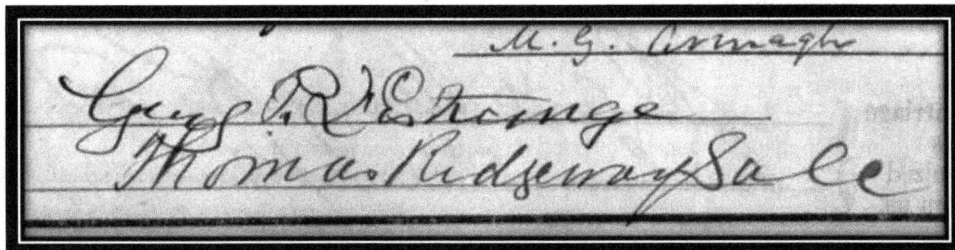

- Thomas Sale & Catherine Unknown

  o Martha Sale – b. Jan 1877, bapt. 1 Feb 1877 (Baptism, **Ballymacelligott & Ballyseedy Parish**)

    (Baptism, **Castleisland Parish**)

Thomas Sale (father):

Residence - Castleisland - February 1, 1877

Occupation - Station Master - February 1, 1877

- Thomas Sale & Honor Flannigan

  o Henry Sale – b. 29 Mar 1837, bapt. 29 Mar 1837 (Baptism, **Causeway Parish** (RC))

  o Ellen Sale – b. 3 Mar 1839, bapt. 3 Mar 1839 (Baptism, **Causeway Parish** (RC))

  o Thomas Sale – b. 16 Nov 1845, bapt. 16 Nov 1845 (Baptism, **Causeway Parish** (RC))

Hurst

Thomas Sale (father):

Residence - Heart Hill - March 29, 1837

March 3, 1839

November 16, 1845

- Thomas Sale & Margaret Slaterry

  - James Sale – b. 11 Jun 1846, bapt. 11 Jun 1846 (Baptism, **Causeway Parish (RC)**)

Thomas Sale (father):

Residence - Heir Hill - June 11, 1846

- Thomas Sale & Mary Dolan

  - Catherine Sale – bapt. 14 Jan 1851 (Baptism, **St. Catherine Parish (RC)**)

- Thomas Sale & Mary Sale

  - Mary Sale – bur. 27 Jan 1636 (Burial, **St. Michan Parish**)

  - Jane Sale – bur. 22 Jun 1643 (Burial, **St. Michan Parish**)

- Thomas Sale & Unknown

  - Thomas Sale & Julia Galvin – 19 Dec 1848 (Marriage, **St. Paul Parish**)

Signatures:

Sale Surname Ireland: 1600s to 1900s

Thomas Sale (son):

    Residence - Royal Barrack - December 19, 1848

    Occupation - Corporal, 3rd Regiment - December 19, 1848

Julia Galvin, daughter of William Galvin (daughter-in-law):

    Residence - Stony Batter - December 19, 1848

    Occupation - Servant - December 19, 1848

William Galvin (father):

    Occupation - Smith

Thomas Sale (father):

    Occupation - Farmer

Wedding Witnesses:

John Wilkinson & Mary Gilroy

Signatures:

Hurst

- Thomas Sale & Unknown

  o Samuel Sale & Rachel Condell, b. 1841, bur. 21 May 1897 – 28 Dec 1866 (Marriage, **Dunleckney Parish**)

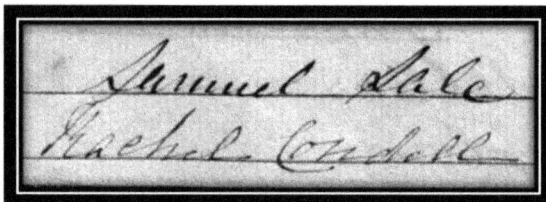

Signatures:

Samuel Sale (son):

    Residence - Ballyhue, Edenderry Parish, King's County - December 28, 1866

    Occupation - Farmer - December 28, 1866

Rachel Condell, daughter of James Condell (daughter-in-law):

    Residence - Rathellin - December 28, 1866

        Leighlinbridge, Rathellin - before May 21, 1897

    Occupation - School Teacher - December 28, 1866

    Age at Death - 56 years

James Condell (father):

    Occupation - Farmer

Thomas Sale (father):

    Occupation - Farmer

Sale Surname Ireland: 1600s to 1900s

Wedding Witnesses:

William Condell & James Condell

Signatures:

- Unknown Sale & Unknown

  o Emily Sale

Signature:

- Unknown Sale & Unknown

  o Emily Sale

Signature:

- Unknown Sale & Unknown

  o Henry Sale

Signature:

- Wallace Sale & Mary Unknown

  o Leonard Sale – bapt. 1754 (Baptism, **St. Andrew Parish** (RC))

- William Sale & Elizabeth Unknown

  o Elizabeth Sale – bapt. 29 Mar 1758 (Baptism, **St. Catherine Parish**)

- William Sale & Mary Connell

  o Catherine Sale – bapt. 16 Jul 1808 (Baptism, **Cork - South Parish** (RC))

William Sale (father):

Residence - Globe Lane - July 16, 1808

- William Sale & Mary Roche

  o Patrick Sale – bapt. Mar 1852 (Baptism, **St. Michan Parish** (RC))

Individual Baptisms/Births

- John Sale – bapt. 9 Jul 1820 (Baptism, **Ballymacelligott & Ballyseedy Parish**)

John Sale (child):

   Remarks about Birth - foundling

Individual Burials

- Anne Sale – bur. 8 Apr 1790 (Burial, **St. Mark Parish**)

- Anne Sophia Sale – b. 1857, d. 28 Oct 1861, bur. Unclear (Burial, **St. James Parish**)

Anne Sophia Sale (deceased):

    Residence - No. 19, Irwin Street - October 28, 1861

    Age at Death - 4 years

- Eleanor Sale – bur. 22 Mar 1791 (Burial, **St. Peter Parish**)

Eleanor Sale (deceased):

    Residence - Kevin's Street - before March 22, 1791

    Place of Burial - Kevin's Cemetery

- Elizabeth Sale – bur. 20 Mar 1640 (Burial, **St. Michan Parish**)

Elizabeth Sale (deceased):

    Also Known As - Elizabeth De La Sale

- Elizabeth Sale – bur. 24 Mar 1764 (Burial, **St. Luke Parish**)

- Elizabeth Sale – b. 1788, bur. 4 Mar 1818 (Burial, **St. Peter Parish**)

Elizabeth Sale (deceased):

    Residence - Fitzwilliam Lane - before March 4, 1818

    Age at Death - 30 years

Sale Surname Ireland: 1600s to 1900s

- George Sale – bur. 22 Oct 1788 (Burial, **St. Paul Parish**)

- George Sale – bur. 18 Jul 1790 (Burial, **St. Paul Parish**)

- George Sale – b. 1864, bur. 19 Jul 1869 (Burial, **Irishtown Parish**)

George Sale (deceased):

    Residence - Ring's End - before July 19, 1869

    Age at Death - 5 years

- Hannah Sale – b. 1795, bur. 10 Oct 1868 (Burial, **Irishtown Parish**)

Hannah Sale (deceased):

    Residence - Ring's End - October 10, 1868

    Age at Death - 73 years

- Hannah Sale – b. May 1856, bur. 28 Oct 1868 (Burial, **Irishtown Parish**)

Hannah Sale (deceased):

    Residence - Ring's End - before October 28, 1868

    Age at Death - 10 ½ years

- Henry Sale – b. 1813, bur. 21 Aug 1815 (Burial, **St. Peter Parish**)

Henry Sale (deceased):

    Age at Death - 2 years

- James Sale – bur. 7 Feb 1717 (Burial, **St. Mary Parish**)

- James Sale – bur. 10 Jun 1791 (Burial, **St. Paul Parish**)

Hurst

- Jane Sale – bur. 17 Apr 1792 (Burial, **St. Paul Parish**)

- John Sale – bur. 1 Sep 1725 (Burial, **St. Catherine Parish**)

John Sale (deceased):

  Age at Death - child

- John Sale – b. 1813, d. 17 Feb 1814, bur. 1814 (Burial, **St. Peter Parish**)

John Sale (deceased):

  Age at Death - 1 year

- John Sale – b. 1815, bur. 16 Sep 1842 (Burial, **St. Mark Parish**)

John Sale (deceased):

  Residence - Fleet Street - before September 16, 1842

  Age at Death - 27 years

- Mary Sale – bur. 1 Oct 1794 (Burial, **St. Catherine Parish**)

Mary Sale (deceased):

  Residence - Thomas Court - before October 1, 1794

- Mary Sale – b. Jun 1844, bur. 4 Aug 1844 (Burial, **St. George Parish**)

Mary Sale (father):

  Residence - 11 Lower Eccles Lane - before August 4, 1844

  Age at Death - 3 months

Sale Surname Ireland: 1600s to 1900s

- Richard Sale – bur. 11 Feb 1793 (Burial, **St. Mark Parish**)

- William Sale – bur. 23 Dec 1729 (Burial, **St. Peter Parish**)

- William Sale – bur. 12 Oct 1746 (Burial, **St. Luke Parish**)

- William Sale – bur. 3 Sep 1749 (Burial, **St. James Parish**)

William Sale (father):

    Residence - Watling Street - before September 3, 1749

Individual Marriages

- Alice Sale & Thomas Owen – 15 Aug 1669 (Marriage, **St. Michan Parish**)

- Amy Constance Sale & Joseph McCabe

  - Mary Elisha McCabe – b. 1 Oct 1893, bapt. 15 Oct 1893 (Baptism, **Rathmines Parish (RC)**)

  - Francis Reginald McCabe – b. 30 Jan 1896, bapt. 12 Feb 1896 (Baptism, **Rathmines Parish (RC)**)

Joseph McCabe (father):

Residence - 4 Homeville - October 15, 1893

February 12, 1896

- Anne Sale & James Nestor

  - James Nestor – bapt. 25 May 1847 (Baptism, **St. Catherine Parish (RC)**)

- Anne Sale & John Neil

  - Julia Neil – bapt. 9 Feb 1835 (Baptism, **St. Nicholas Parish (RC)**)

  - John Neil – bapt. 1847 (Baptism, **St. Mary Parish (RC)**)

  - Margaret Neil – bapt. 1849 (Baptism, **St. Mary Parish (RC)**)

- Catherine Sale & David Keeffe – 6 Jun 1852 (Marriage, **Carrigaline & Templebrigid Parish (RC)**)

Wedding Witnesses:

William Daly & Maurice Mahony

Sale Surname Ireland: 1600s to 1900s

- Catherine Sale & Lawrence Connell

  o Catherine Connell – b. 1 Jun 1858, bapt. 11 June 1858 (Baptism, **St. Nicholas Parish** (RC))

Lawrence Connell (father):

Residence - Coombe Hospital - June 11, 1858

- Catherine Sale & Richard Lumach (L u m a c h)

  o Daniel Patrick Lumach (L u m a c h) – b. 5 Mar 1888, bapt. 8 Mar 1888 (Baptism, **St. Agatha Parish** (RC))

Richard Lumach (father):

Residence - 8 Newcomen Avenue - March 8, 1888

- Cecelia Sale & Martin Grant

  o Marcella Grant – b. 1897, bapt. 1897 (Baptism, **St. Andrew Parish** (RC))

  o Joseph Grant – b. 1899, bapt. 1899 (Baptism, **St. Andrew Parish** (RC))

  o Richard Grant – b. 1902, bapt. 1902 (Baptism, **St. Andrew Parish** (RC))

Martin Grant (father):

Residence - 24 Clarence Street - 1897

Holles Hospital - 1899

1902

- Eleanor Sale & Matthew Hiney

  o John Hiney – bapt. 21 Nov 1744 (Baptism, **St. Catherine Parish** (RC))

Hurst

- Eleanor Sale & Maurice O'Brien

    o George O'Brien – bapt. 31 Aug 1849 (Baptism, **St. Nicholas Parish (RC)**)

    o Maurice O'Brien – b. 4 Mar 1854, bapt. 8 Mar 1854 (Baptism, **St. Nicholas Parish (RC)**)

Martin O'Brien (father):

Residence - 5 New Market - March 8, 1854

- Elizabeth Sale & Christopher Byrne (B y r n e) – 6 Nov 1807 (Marriage, **St. Andrew Parish (RC)**)

Wedding Witnesses:

Richard Byrne & Mary Ellis

- Elizabeth Sale & Henry Burin

    o Henry Burin – b. 1902, bapt. 1902 (Baptism, **St. Andrew Parish (RC)**)

Henry Burin (father):

Residence - Holles Street Hospital - 1902

- Elizabeth Sale & Richard Colley – 23 Dec 1719 (Marriage, **St. Anne Parish**)

- Elizabeth Sale & William Beys – 4 Oct 1829 (Marriage, **St. Mark Parish**)

Signatures:

Sale Surname Ireland: 1600s to 1900s

Elizabeth Sale (wife):

    Residence - St. Mark Parish - October 4, 1829

William Beys (husband):

    Residence - North Yarmouth, Norfolk, England - October 4, 1829

    Occupation - Mariner - October 4, 1829

Wedding Witnesses:

Thomas Edmonds & Michael Singleton

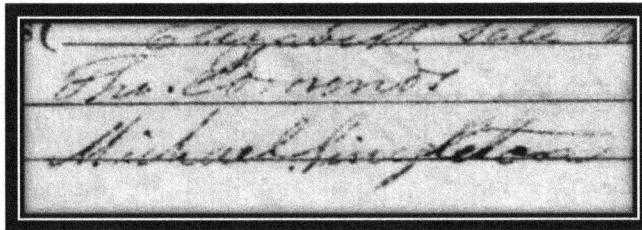

Signatures:

- Ellen Sale & Timothy McClure

  o Mary McClure – b. 6 Mar 1868, bapt. 8 Mar 1868 (Baptism, **Causeway Parish (RC)**)

Timothy McClure (father):

    Residence - Lacca - March 8, 1868

- Hannah Sale & Jeremiah McCarthy

  o Timothy McCarthy – bapt. 31 Aug 1834 (Baptism, **Cork - South Parish (RC)**)

- Harriet Sale & Henry Williams – Unclear (Marriage, **Sandford Parish**)

- Jane Sale & John McDermott (M c D e r m o t t)

  o Joseph Gulielmo McDermott (M c D e r m o t t) – b. 15 Apr 1858, bapt. 19 Apr 1858 (Baptism, **St. Mary, Pro Cathedral Parish (RC)**)

Hurst

John McDermott (father):

Residence - 14 Langrish Place - April 19, 1858

- Jane Sale & Maurice Galvan
  - James Galvan – b. 16 Feb 1876, bapt. 16 Feb 1887 (Baptism, **Ballybunion Parish (RC)**)
  - Jeremiah Galvan – b. 8 Dec 1876, bapt. 8 Dec 1876 (Baptism, **Ballybunion Parish (RC)**)

Maurice Galvan (father):

Residence - Gale Hill - December 8, 1876

Glouria - February 16, 1887

- Jane Sale & Nicholas McCormick (M c C o r m i c k) – 19 Nov 1753 (Marriage, **St. Audoen Parish (RC)**)

Wedding Witnesses:

John Mary McCormick & Margaret McCormick

- Jane Sale & Thomas D'Arcy
  - James D'Arcy – b. 1892, bapt. 1892 (Baptism, **St. Andrew Parish (RC)**)

Thomas D'Arcy (father):

Residence - 27 Cumberland Street - 1892

- Jane Sale & Thomas Hogan
  - Anne Hogan – b. 17 Jan 1869, bapt. 27 Jan 1869 (Baptism, **St. Mary, Pro Cathedral Parish (RC)**)

Thomas Hogan (father):

Residence - 15 Mabbot Street - January 27, 1869

Sale Surname Ireland: 1600s to 1900s

- Martha Sale & John Butler

  - Anne Jane Butler – b. 11 Oct 1863, bapt. 23 Nov 1863 (Baptism, **St. Nicholas Parish** (RC))

John Butler (father):

Residence - 110 Francis Street - November 23, 1863

- Martha Sale & Samuel Rotheram – 18 Jun 1778 (Marriage, **St. Anne Parish**)

- Mary Sale & George Blunt

  - Gulielmo Blunt – b. 13 May 1836, bapt. 20 Jun 1859 (Baptism, **St. Lawrence Parish** (RC))

George Blunt (father):

Residence - 3 Upper Mayor Street - June 20, 1859

- Mary Sale & Mark Maguire – 7 Feb 1823 (Marriage, **St. Andrew Parish** (RC))

Wedding Witnesses:

Jeanne Kelly & Margaret Traynor

- Mary Sale & Michael Healy

  - Mary Healy – b. 26 Dec 1880, bapt. 26 Dec 1880 (Baptism, **Listowel Parish** (RC))

  - Honor Healy – b. 15 Jul 1882, bapt. 15 Jul 1882 (Baptism, **Listowel Parish** (RC))

  - Bridget Healy – b. 9 Jul 1884, bapt. 13 Jul 1884 (Baptism, **Listowel Parish** (RC))

  - John Healy – b. 25 Jan 1886, bapt. 27 Jan 1886 (Baptism, **Listowel Parish** (RC))

  - Thomas Healy – b. 13 Apr 1887, bapt. 13 Apr 1887 (Baptism, **Listowel Parish** (RC))

  - Michael Healy – b. 28 Oct 1888, bapt. 28 Oct 1888 (Baptism, **Listowel Parish** (RC))

  - Joan Healy – b. 11 Sep 1892, bapt. 11 Sep 1892 (Baptism, **Listowel Parish** (RC))

  - Margaret Healy – b. 17 May 1895, bapt. 17 May 1895 (Baptism, **Listowel Parish** (RC))

Hurst

- o Maurice Healy – b. 13 Nov 1896, bapt. 15 Nov 1896 (Baptism, **Listowel Parish** (RC))

- o Margaret Healy – b. 18 Oct 1898, bapt. 23 Oct 1898 (Baptism, **Listowel Parish** (RC))

- o Catherine Healy – b. 7 May 1900, bapt. 13 May 1900 (Baptism, **Listowel Parish** (RC))

Michael Healy (father):

Residence - Clievragh - December 26, 1880

July 15, 1882

July 13, 1884

January 27, 1886

April 13, 1887

October 28, 1888

November 15, 1896

October 23, 1898

May 13, 1900

Listowel - September 11, 1892

- • Mary Sale & Michael Mellon

- o Peter Mellon – b. 1899, bapt. 1899 (Baptism, **St. Andrew Parish** (RC))

Michael Mellon (father):

Residence - Holles Street Hospital - 1899

Sale Surname Ireland: 1600s to 1900s

- Mary Sale & Michael Shea

  - Daniel Shea – bapt. 1859 (Baptism, **St. Mary Parish** (RC))

  - Michael Shea – bapt. 1860 (Baptism, **St. Mary Parish** (RC))

  - Elizabeth Shea – bapt. 1862 (Baptism, **St. Mary Parish** (RC))

  - Elizabeth Shea – bapt. 1865 (Baptism, **St. Mary Parish** (RC))

  - Patrick Shea – b. 1869, bapt. 1869 (Baptism, **St. Mary Parish** (RC))

- Mary Sale & Roger Quinlan

  - Roger Quinlan – b. 17 May 1844, bapt. 17 May 1844 (Baptism, **Causeway Parish** (RC))

Roger Quinlan (father):

Residence - Heart Hill - May 17, 1844

- Mary Sale & Thomas Gregory – 7 Apr 1811 (Marriage, **St. Mary, Pro Cathedral Parish** (RC))

Wedding Witnesses:

Matthew Collins & Catherine Ward

- Mary Sale & Timothy McCarthy

  - Jane McCarthy – b. 13 Nov 1836, bapt. 13 Nov 1836 (Baptism, **Causeway Parish** (RC))

Timothy McCarthy (father):

Residence - Dromartin - November 13, 1836

- Mary Sale & William Nagle – 6 May 1858 (Marriage, **St. Mary Parish** (RC))

  - Michael Nagle – bapt. 1859 (Baptism, **St. Mary Parish** (RC))

Wedding Witnesses:

John Nagle & Unknown Duggan

Hurst

- Mary A. Sale & Andrew Owen – 8 Apr 1861 (Marriage, **St. Mary Parish (RC)**)

Wedding Witnesses:

Dennis Byrne & Esther Whelan

- Rebecca Sale & Joseph Penderd – 8 Jul 1750 (Marriage, **St. Bride Parish**)

Joseph Penderd (husband):

   Occupation - Esquire - July 8, 1750

Sale Surname Ireland: 1600s to 1900s

Name Variations

Includes Latin and Abbreviated forms of names found in the original documents.

Abigail = Abigale, Abigall

Anne = Ann, Anna, Annae

Bartholomew = Barth, Bartholmeus, Bartholomeo

Bridget = Birgis, Brigid, Brigida, Bridgit

Catherine = Catharine, Catharina, Catharinae, Catherina, Cath, Catha, Cathae, Cathe, Cathn, Kate

Charles = Carolus, Charls, Chas

Christopher = Christoph

Daniel = Danielem, Danielis

Edmund = Edmond

Edward = Ed, Edwd

Eleanor = Eleo, Eleonora, Elinor, Ellenor

Elizabeth = Betty, Elisa, Elisabeth, Eliz, Eliza, Elizab, Elizh, Elizth

Ellen = Elena, Ellena

Emily = Emilia

Esther = Essie, Ester

Francis = Fransicum

George = Geo, Georg, Georgius

Grace = Gratiae

Gulielmo = Guil, Guillelmi, Gulielmum, Guillelmus, Gulmi

Helen = Helena

Sale Surname Ireland: 1600s to 1900s

Honor = Hanora, Honora

James = Jacobi, Jacobus, Jas

Jane = Joanna

Jeanne = Jeannae, Joannae

Joan = Johanna, Joney

John = Jno, Joannem, Joannes, Johannis

Joseph = Jos

Juliana = Julian

Leticia = Letitia, Lettice, Letticia

Lewis = Louis

Luke = Lucas

Margaret = Margarita, Margaritae, Margeret, Marget, Margt

Martha = Marthae

Mary = Maria, My

Mary Anne = Marianna, Marianne, Maryanne

Michael = Michaelis, Michl

Patrick = Pat, Patt, Patk, Patricii, Patricius

Peter = Petri

Richard = Ricardi, Ricardus, Rich, Richd

Robert = Roberti

Rose = Rosa, Rosae

Thomas = Thom, Thomae, Thoms, Thos, Ths

Timothy = Timotheus, Timy

William = Wil, Will, Willm, Wm

Notes

Notes

Notes

Notes

Notes

Notes

Index

B

Barrett

C

Hurst

Hurst

W

Walsh

About The Author

Donovan Hurst graduated from San Diego State University with a Bachelor of Arts in the major field of studies of History and a minor in the field of studies of Anthropology. He is a current member of The General Society of Mayflower Descendants and has been conducting genealogical research for over 10 years tracing back his ancestors to their ancestral homelands in Denmark, England, France, Germany, Ireland, Norway, and Scotland.